MW01289677

This book belongs to the future

Mrs. ________________

Made in the USA
Las Vegas, NV
23 October 2021

32920937R00059